Bad Daughter

Also by Sarah Gorham

The Cure (2003)
The Tension Zone (1996)
Don't Go Back to Sleep (1989)

Last Call: Poems on Alcoholism, Addiction, and Deliverance (1997),
edited with Jeffrey Skinner

Bad Daughter

SARAH GORHAM

Four Way Books
Tribeca

Please direct all inquiries to:
Editorial Office
Four Way Books
POB 535, Village Station
New York, NY 10014
www.fourwaybooks.com

Library of Congress Cataloging-in-Publication Data

Gorham, Sarah, 1954-
 Bad daughter : poems / by Sarah Gorham.
    p. cm.
 Poems.
 ISBN 978-1-935536-16-1 (pbk. : alk. paper)
 I. Title.
 PS3557.O7554B33 2011
 811'.54--dc22

                              2011004084

This book is manufactured in the United States of America
and printed on acid-free paper.

Four Way Books is a not-for-profit literary press. We are grateful for the assistance
we receive from individual donors, public arts agencies, and private foundations.

This publication is made possible with public funds
from the New York State Council on the Arts, a state agency.

Distributed by University Press of New England
One Court Street, Lebanon, NH 03766

[clmp] We are a proud member of the Council of Literary Magazines and Presses.

Contents

III.

For

Nancy, Kim, Jenny, Beckie

Laura, Bonnie

Lucille, Josephine

I.

In all desire to know there is already a drop of cruelty.

—Nietzsche

Bust of a Young Girl in the Snow

Odd place for a sculpture—
cemented to a newel post
on the front porch,
disarming the winter visitor
who wanted a good grip
and not this unsettling head
floating waist high.

Lips apart, ear like a split
oyster, rough erosion
crawling up her nape
and, over the cheek,
a verdigris birthmark.
Thankfully, her metal's

well beyond cold.
Souls may be stored
on planets, said Plato,
each of them mindfully
sowed in a star.
I think there's a live one
in every snowflake

falling for a shoulder,
the tip of a warm tongue,
better life in the new
world. They accumulate
on the child's brow,
her bowl-cropped hair,
tarnished dimple and fold

of neckskin. They bunch up
on her Northeast side
like shivering immigrants.
The result is something to behold—
an elephant girl, a misshapen,
Phantom of the Opera mask
covering half her motionless face.

How often resurrection's
a slight miscalculation
of past, present, and future.
A cow nudging its dead
calf. A little girl's eyes
in winter,
opened rigid and wide.

When we were good we were...

precise, mindful of our tools.
Spent more time sharpening than making the cut.
Made wind chimes from sewing needles
and laid the broken ones gently to rest
in pillboxes. Without birds and their
thread-like courses, trees, we believed,
might float upwards. We tied little silk knots
to measure our way. Scoured the dirty parts
with lemons and gardenia spray.

When we were bad, we were extravagant
like cruise ships through a canal.
We improvised, lied, crayoned
all over each other. We lost knives
or left them to rust, stepped on discarded needles
and blamed someone else.
Birds scolded from above as our dog
went rolling, rolling, rolling in horseshit.
It felt so good, so incredibly green.

Immortality

The baby is a drug, for she makes us hungry and delirious.

Have you seen the uncles shake their faces like monkeys,
      lips floppy and moist, saliva flying?

The eyes of the baby are lucky nickels in a row.
      But your age has you bound, your sadness a woolen sari.

You are full of stirs and folds, whips and dark layers.

How might you approach the baby? Not with desire,
      nor entitlement or castle armaments of teeth.

Make yourself small. The baby is an Alice-in-Wonderland door,
      tiny beneath the hedges.

She is naked, skin like spun sugar, fingers pink fiddleheads.
      Remember when the names for little things weren't sickening?

Touch that fantastic little foot. The baby is an implant, a fresh cutting.
      She will take. She will take you away.

Birthday

In the dim before, I saw a colt
edge towards the road. My body clamor
was like that steely road forbidding,
no, bidding her home.

Hands about were powdered
beneath their gloves though mine
were sweating the turn, blind turn
to carry her home.

I held my tongue while others
placed their bets, too much
of me already committed
to call this fun. And then, god bless,

the bright occurrence: our colt
cast out one hoof and then
all four. The gates flew open;
she galloped home.

Doppelgänger

Once there was a girl,
Shy Violet

also known as *Sky Violence,*
who tied her saintly

siblings to the banister
with father's satin neckties

and curled their saintly hair
with library paste and paper clips

and painted on their lips
scarlet inner-tubes.

Then laughed uproariously
and unlatched the bunny cages

to set all hoppers free,
loosening a hurricane,

closet hangers clanging,
screen doors whapping,

summoning their mother
of pencil skirts

and happy family theory
her mouth a sideways sprig

of olive tree. *Where
are your manners,* little flower?

What on earth have you done?

Prick and Twinge

The needle snapped in two, slipped into her heel
with hardly a bruise. *An obvious ploy*, mother thought,
glancing at the placid skin. So off the little girl limped
and built a shelf made of Kleenex into her dusty
Beatles shoe. The pain was bearable, so long as she was
never barefoot, never wore patent leather party shoes again.

After a time, the foot stank, so mother hunted down
an icy fungus gel. She saw a crimson line,
death infection streaking up her daughter's ankle.
Boom, they were in a race car, breaking all the rules,
mother swearing, *You fool, you big terrible fool*, though
reassuring with a pat, *I'm not talking about you, honey.*

Daughter knew, but still felt foolish, as if she'd let
the water run to overflow. Inside the doctor's house
a roaring fire, rock candy in a medicine jar. He was blunt,
How did this happen? An intelligent woman like you?
then thrust his hand into the fire and singed the tweezers
blue. He swabbed her heel and dug the needle out (no Novocain).

My only day off, he rued, and mother flushed bright,
far more than the little girl bargained for—
the color of mama's love, mixed with shame.

Electret

charges of equal magnitude but opposite sign

No

to the cat she treasured yes
for its missing eye.

No

to the party shrimp yes
because her mouth watered.

Not now

to the rope swing, yes now
oh please

Not yet

lick of sour cream then when

This first

spelling quiz, shower, dishes no way
it's your responsibility

And then

say sorry to your sister what for

Too young

that swallow of wine not true
though it might give her parents rest

Straight to bed

wouldn't let them sleep, not tired
or kiss or think

High Tea

For the family served, one by one. For Margaret to raise a spoon,
quivering while her chocolate steamed.

Where's Nick? Notch, groove, slit, from the French, for *niche*.

For Grandpa, a Horace Fletcher fan, each bite ripped and ground,
at the very least, thirty times.

Please wait.

(I dare you to kick her shin. I dare you. She's kicking me.
She's a stupid ass. You're a stupid ass.)

No fighting. There's been a death.

For second helpings, for the plates clattering and scraped.
For more waiting, our bodies like the itchy center of the sun.

Nick. A pocket knife, we think . . .

Nick: to steal, catch unawares. The critical moment, slashed,
scored on a tally stick.

Someone may have murdered him.

For the crumbs swept into a bowl. For the napkins folded and piled.
Chairs squealing, candles blown.

There'll be an investigation. Your mouth . . . wait

The linen stiff, the weep forbidden.

Soakaway

Reverse well, a hole in the ground
that seeps rather than contains.
Spell of pain that permeates
the heaviest clay. For caution,
surround it with crime tape.
We know how well that holds;
nothing draws us in like yellow.
So—why not savor the drain,
the "S" sound of sinking waste.
Imagine a sunset, lavender and red
as battered morals, the underworld
eager to drink.

Salon

She sat before a "hair technician" who talked with his hands, that is,
he wasn't paying attention to her hair, which he parted and sheaved
and tied into a dozen tiny bundles.

To discourage deer or other animals, scatter hair around your garden.

Imagine her scalp sowed with rice seedlings, blonde shoots
shaped like Ys, bound with purple rubber bands.

Worse than a hair in your soup, is a long one pulled
from a bite of meat.

She was polite, though the man wasn't worth it, and foul water
stirred under her "nice" membrane.

Hair is an outgrowth of dead skin, keratins, proteins, chains
of amino acids also found in hooves, feathers, teeth.

It was her first dance, first date, first time she had her hair done.
She stood in the shower, distraught, ripping out the little plants.

That it continues to grow after death is a myth.

She thought she would die, would rather be dead than dance
with such hair.

It is true when a girl sinks, her hair spreads like a flower,
the last of her to go under.

Barbecue

Is it progress if a cannibal uses a fork?
When she held up her fork,
she saw family: four tines,

three, two, one. Sisters—they were that close,
jockeying for love in a cage
with silver bars. *The origin of the fork*

was a spear in an animal's heart.
You've heard of knife scars
on a plate? Blame it on the knife,

though the fork held the weakling down.
Chicken back or wing, maybe two—
and always the wait, sisters . . .

Tonight she would mind
her parents' appeal for peace,
place her knife back on the table,

though her left hand still clung
to the fork.

Ice Storm

Hear it fall, laughter from a train.
Under the transparent tapping,
crawl into a hollow
sleep. First comes a dream
of cocktail banter. Then crazy
clappers in a grange hall.
It makes her sad, this uncalled for
enthusiasm. Answers unlink
and veer from their questions.
Deer blink under the dangerous wires.
Now is not the time to hope
in the smoke of night, in deep
dying boughs. She cannot feel her hands
nor find her serious throat.

Passeggiata

Her mother on the cell phone.
Flight 3260 arriving soon, or the bridge is up
and a yacht slithers by ever-so-slowly or
she needs to use up those long distance units.
Here's a minute or two to touch base.
HELLO DEAR. I'M ON MY WAY TO PARIS
(OR MY DANCING LESSON OR MAINE OR TENNIS).
I'VE ONLY A SECOND. TELL ME ABOUT YOURSELF.
ARE YOU STILL TAKING LATIN? STUDYING HARD?
WHAT ELSE—THAT POLYSCI CLASS YOU HATED SO MUCH.
FEELINGS CHANGED AT ALL? STILL THINK 8 1/2
IS FELLINI'S BEST? HOW'S THAT YOUNG MAN OF YOURS—
RYAN— WAS THAT HIS NAME? Even face to face
over a five course meal, her mother's arsenal
of questions that once seemed so flattering—
doesn't a girl love to talk about herself?—
now merely mystifies. *Just who is this person*
so interested in me. Or is it duty,
or intellectual research, or . . . something.

                                     If she were honest
the girl would mention not-so-terrific
developments, that she switched to bunny courses,
one called "Subways and Bridges" and fulfilled
her PE credits with "Ultimate" and "Independent
Running." That she forgets to show up for these
and hasn't held down a single part-time job—
not groceries, not temping, not even ice cream.
She spends her evenings rollerblading
deep into Amish country, where the boys
stand around like stumps, where chickens

18

have weird, furry legs. She's a gorgeous
dream to them, speck of neon light, Tinkerbell
streaking across the sky. It's in the genes—
travelers can get away with anything,
and never die.

Scaffold for a Sonnet

Your clothes
spread
across the floor.

Good citizen—
hang them
by their shoulders.

It is not true
a poem
must police;

but a rose
fastened
to a lattice

arrests
the sun.

We Are Bold to Say

Our father who art for children
a speckled man

hollowed be thy name with spoon
and woodcarver's tool

colored as we wish red blue violet
a crayon book thy kingdom

come thy will be done
grown-ups self-effaced as in

best-behavior airplane crashes
or if no one survives

on our way to heaven yes
give us this day our daily bread

our animal crackers and soup
forget not animals bugs trees

and forgive us our trespass
on next-door lawns

retrieving just one soccer ball
as we forgive those

on our grass lead us
not into the public gardens

where we may be tempted
unfrocked beneath a basswood tree

but deliver us from the evil
of bitter teachers mushrooms

cold for thine is the kingdom
the power the glory—our region

of skyscrapers and earthly kings
feels like forever

compared to our visits with You

Floaters

Dark nothings follow your touch,
tickle your salt, untie your shoes.

Distant and intimate, swallows
above a lake, fruit flies in an apple's bruise.

Night is their green room
and morning their slippery stage.

A mere blink sweeps them away,
but they return, for their verb

is "to meddle." Like sweat bees
or hawks, they pursue a sour scent.

They are the unnumbered,
unlisted commandments.

The fear in a mother's voice
that you'll never be useful or clean.

The end of illness is the end of metaphor

She was the pebble in the soldier's shoe,
hunger that hardens into stone.

She was the baby of a large man
in the body of a tiny woman.

Her will was a watermelon
wedged into a garden hose.

She'd always be like this,
always disagreeable, always alone.

Then one morning, a sliver of hope:
she watched a tooth disintegrate

inside a glass of Coke.
Drink this, someone said,

and thus commenced her dream:
the stone began to crumble,

melt like a chicken bouillon cube.
A pebble could be made into soup!

Enough for her *and* the soldier,
officers, the entire village, even.

No one would ever go hungry again!
The End.

Our House

Mother was
  a waterfall at night,

a pewter eye.
  The moon

between her fingers
  half in or out of sight.

Mother was a moth
  who tried to settle on the water,

held fast to the bedroom wall.
  Four children

stirred the pool,
  made a school of pike,

a choppy wake.
  Once or twice

a hound dog growled,
  dipped his big brown paw

into the stream, almost leapt;
  a threshold

is the place to pause.

II.

What the daughter does, the mother did.

—Jewish Proverb

Sixteen

Tangerine was her truth
and tangerine her hair
and many were the toughies
who backed into her fire.

Most were but flickers
that lifted her to smoke,
the one I grew to care about
she burned with lines of coke.

Then glanced a tangerine glower
and shed an orange pride
and conjured the toughest boy of all
to push my love aside.

The Sacrifice

Memory is a ditzy court reporter:

You swear she was a good girl, the perfect

little lady, though her cruelty,

you admit, awoke

just as the day ended.

Now you shuffle your debts

in order to appease her.

You shake out your clothes

and pennies like a dozen

sad-faced clowns

glower from the floor.

Whatever can you do, when

so many bright collection agents

burn at the periphery?

An invoice has been found.

The sacrifice you pretend to love.

After Pindar

Sarah of *sear* which is burning, and of *Ra*, eye that rises phoenix-like
each morning. Sarah like *saracen* or *sarakenos,* Eastern god of sunrise.
Sarah of *seer* and of *rah rah rah,* who saw through with her golden
eye, and applauded. Sarah the queen, *sherratu,* that is, she ruled, as in
you rule, dude, but not without fear. Sarah close to *sehr,* German for
very, as in exaggerated, and of *hreaw* or raw, that is, tender-uncooked-
thick-blooded-thin-skinned. A sound like *sarà,* from the Italian *Che
sarà, sarà,* though she dislikes inaction. Sarah a toiler, a thinker, a queen
in contemplation of unsightly things, such as the earth cast in shadow,
or frost, or herself, singed.

Accommodation

To the weak I become weak.

To the rich I speak of my uncle
with his ranch and million-dollar townhouse.

To nonbelievers I am silent.

I sing along with the Beatles, no matter how excellent my book,
my prayer, my brochure.

To my child I became my mother, and her mother, and hers.

I have a soft spot for the handicapped
right in the middle of my skull.

To my husband I'm capable, for he is incapable
and were he capable I would not know what to do with myself.

To the Jew I'm half Jew, though truthfully on my father's side.

I wear black in New York, white in the Keys,
rust-brown in New Mexico.

To the poor I tell the story of my bicycle.

I surrender to the rain,
but only during a long long walk.

To me, a snake looks like a river, a river
shaped by compromise.

To my priest I'm all ears and servitude,
especially when she is watching me.

To God I am soft tissue, blood, milk,
erratic love.

Vague

When I say *oolong*, you hear *how long*.
Oh the vagaries of biology: histaminic tongue, water in the ear.

Or am I drowned out, this ear-splitting, shuffle tape
flinging us like vagabonds from 17th century Vienna
to Virginia to India, where they grew, and still grow, a musky oolong.

The vagus nerve saunters around heart, lungs, mouth, sweat glands,
outer ear, and still delivers, despite its broad job description.

Which kind? Of oolong? Indeed. The color amber,
which melts or warbles or signals *slow, slow, slow.*

I love the precise way men reach for their wallets
in their jeans, back pocket, as if they had eyes . . . *How much?*

Said Borges: No use counting the days like dollars.

When you ask for the time, it depends. *You mean right now?* (Yogi Berra)
My watch like a vagrant refuses to be pinned down.

Money is determining. This oolong, vacuum-packed and shipped
by the Behera Brothers: $11.89 a heap.

But how many leaves make a heap?

You Bother Me

Grackles rise, followed by boat-
tails and the littlest brown jobs.
So much for suet which lures the cat,
then hound-dogs who badger
the groundhog too. *Baroo, baroo.*
How many irritations make a hole
(whole)? The road stumbles
over a root wedge and forever trucks
aggravate the error. Today's special
is Todd on the rocks, with a twist,
battering a hydraulic hammer.
His backyard deck slows, grows,
slows. What is progress
but a deer chased through the forest
by Slovakian curses? What is sailing
but a boat vexed by a wailing
stream of air?

Envy

for Leslie

White horse with his nose in the grass.
Horse finished trying. Acres
of cash and prizes.
Fat horse, couch horse, dirty
pillow horse. Someone *please*
throw those pillows away!
I'll give him a love.
Here horsey, horsey. Only one thing
between me and that horse,
standing in,
standing in a blonde field
of whole rye flour, like freckles
on pale Irish skin, like rich
Irish linen. Dangerous field. Acres
of fat and laziness,
heaven-too-soon.
Do not walk or thrust.
OK to look but don't touch. Seeds
will latch on, scrimshaw in.
Why them and not me.
Why not me. Oh, why not.

Prayer during a Fast

I confess that I have
sinned against you
by what I have eaten
and by what I have
not left uneaten.
In my thirst for a beer,
in my word broken each day
before the ripe banana
sweet roll and cheese,
in the pleasure I receive
from food and, rarely,
the charitable deed.
I have not loved you
with my whole body
not even my aching heart
which can be consoled
only with chocolate.
I have not loved my hunger,
cannot imagine its good.
I am truly sorry
and humbly repent.
I'm an embarrassment
of flesh, so
beneath you. I beseech you—
do not abhor me.
In the name of your Son,
who fasted and prayed
and was betrayed.

Red Mulberry

Imagine a basket, a pottle for mulberries.
A dozen whorled limbs from the middle,
a dozen puppies and only one nipple—
neat-looking, but very unstable.
The Earl of Wind has been known to say,
I love my trees, but not as much as fire.
Of course he blew sideways;
of course the rain ran horizontal.
With a whip and a crack and an awful
angle, he chopped off two branches.
I touched their insides. They were spongy,
like halvah. I myself am
not yet made of honeycomb.
My joints pop and crackle, but do not snap.
Half of me is mighty irritated, Mulberry.
What a waste of proper nutrients, perfect air.
The other half weeps at the fractured
shins of the two thieves.

Homesickness

On another continent, mother circles the farmhouse.
She steams gnocci, tosses them in butter.

Mother and daughter have matching teeth, like a zipper.

If daughter flies home she'll lose eight hours. If her car were amphibious,
the loss would be hardly perceptible.

There's always the mail. And the cell phone, like a human cowbell.
Especially if you are loved.

Mother rings her from the bus stop, train station, grocery store.
When it's time to pay, she says *hang on*. The bus pulls up, gotta go, so long!

Emotion: from the Latin *emovere*—to move away, "in transport."

How would a jet land in the country, gravel roads
and all those electric fences?

She opens her mail, a blue mountain of *Mit Luftpost, Par Avion.*

Genes are a kind of blue letter from a mother
to her daughter: Good news, bad news.

What is a mother but a tooth's way of producing another tooth?

Floater

wayward ash delinquent one
fly-casting on my lens

nauseous thought
like a hair stuck to baby's plate

you plague and dominate the air
with wild sashaying chair to chair

no wiping, whacking
smearing on the ice-encrusted grass

dim corner of mind
reserved for guilt and error

you hide and seek you holy terror
there is no private anywhere

Pounce

So I raced, tumbled, and fell into the sun.
Slid under a birdbath, the very safebox of *pleasant*
where pigeons splashed, revealing their plans
to levitate the world. I joined them, galloping from inner space—

like outer, but gated. I dove right in, instantly charitable,
donating all my favorite games and brightly-boxed
little nothings. I was royalty to them, a silly sheepdog
covered with ticks and fur mosaics. My growlings, well,

call them *endearments*. We held a downright liberal picnic,
right there, plashing in the sun. I ate them one by one.
Then lay back under the feather-dusted sky, pondering.
I had to admit the taste was not so pleasant, really.

Tin Drumming

Autumn loves to insinuate
with the stuck wheel and mud

sucking up your leather boot.
The scent of snow implies the story

of ash, tumble of spent shells.
Easy to foretell this bleak unfolding

if you are scary little Oskar
with his drum and glass-shattering scream.

If not, and you have a little night vision,
imagine porcupines and digger

bees, imagine winter is for dreamers,
and drums are meant for waking them.

After the Accident

1. Pre-Registration

What is your full name?
Your date of birth?
Look at me, am I holding up two or three fingers?
Who should we name as a friend or relative?
Where does your red hair come from? Are you always this thin?
Tell us about your surgeries, even minor.
What makes you most anxious: cancer, mother's diabetes,
or father's alcoholism?
Would you care to file a claim against your parents?
Have you ever tripped, broken a bone, fallen on hard times?
What kind of insurance do you have? Secondary? Mercenary?
Have you ever fired a gun? Been arrested for a crime?
I'm going to take some blood, just a bit.
We can tell a lot from a drop. You're going to feel a stick.
Your signature here, here, and please initial here.
Let me just put this around your wrist.
Have a seat, the doctor will see you.

2. *Wallet Card*

Not deaf not contagious lost control
on the curve gravel rolled skid on
my side broke seven ribs incisors
lower jaw no cars involved don't
remember much tell you the truth
sure could use something for the
pain

3. *Thoracotomy*

Old blood adhering to a lung—
like shaving a balloon, surgeon said.

Three incisions to enter, three to drain.
To make it safe, he'll draw out air,

deflate as you would a hot air
balloon. The count begins from ten.

I wake on cue, dazed, connected
to a fluid bank, brand name

Oasis. Surgeon holds
two photographs: before, after.

Here's what I looked like then—
snarl of crimson spider webs,

then, tidiness. He's clearly proud.
But I'll say this: a cluster of balloons

does not make a party,
just a bunch of doctors, lolling.

4. *Wound Care*

Nurse makes a whistling sound
she summons a saline wash
I feel rain accelerated air
no choice but to lie there
till a pool forms
surrounded by salt heaps
I fear the caving in the rush
of tissue to a drowning fear
broad spectrum microbes
like dental tools arrayed
a diversity of bird beaks
skin flap held back
by a dab of petrolatum mornings
I unwrap the white gauze
stained orange-pink
my leaking thought
patterns the front passes
without warning nurse summons me
to fresh air to make sure I
get out there expose myself

5. How Young Do You Feel on the Inside?

After the accident I gave up
helmets, bikes, scented
flower country and flashes
of gully cool—
had the sick-person dream:
kite tail pulled, slowly, slowly
from my mouth like a magician's
scarf, necklace of silk charms:
feather, lily, sweet licorice
tied in a Revo knot,
finally the snout
of a pet gecko then stop
stop tugging, for its sepia
shadow wriggled under my breast,
some vital organ could be
snagged, leave me torn
like velvet inside a violin case
the instrument itself
vanished.

Loose Thread

Herons fly,
legs dangling above the smoke.

We laminate, we particle-board the cold.

Someone is sobbing in Red Lobster.
Doctor removes a bone from her throat.

We blacktop, we stucco over the mold.

Everyone loves a balloon ride, its tie-up
black, a shrimp's digestive vein.

For every object in the universe
a skein that will unfold.

Go not into the night darling
forward with your slip hanging.

III.

Researchers have found that certain cells escape from a fetus, persisting in the mother's bloodstream decades after she is pregnant. These cells migrate to wounds in the mother's body.

Follow

If you follow the dog into slumber,
you'll find an oval of grass.

The path of a deer will be bald,
like a vein. Dog, shadow, track, trace—

For a body to rise and follow
the ego must be disciplined. Tear off your name,

confess your desire for full-going.
No sleep-walking!

To follow is to serve,
go with, as: a flight attendant.

Follow thy faire sunne, unhappy shaddowe.
Why does no one attend the dead,

their bodies ascending the blackberry ravine?
Because they serve "the light,"

no wish to leave a path
of crumbs, socks, or subway tokens.

I hold my daughter's hair like a dog's lead.
"Now you follow *me*," she cries.

Sigh

Sin, forgiveness: Byron named the bridge between

Ponte dei Sospiri for the watery reprieve

before the blade. Resignation, exasperation,

we sigh to slow the heart,

to scour the tiniest alveoli, and unbind the deep.

A sigh is meaning-full, like an ocean breeze

thick with salt. Nothing to be done, nowhere to go.

Inhale, exhale. Infants sigh in a loop,

a breath allemande left. Your sigh's

comma-shaped, an air mustache, curling at its tips.

What you wanted to say, would have, should have.

The dog collapses on the floor, skin like a dropped rope.

The terrible happens, no, worse . . . .

We sigh alone in a room, parenthetically.

The milky objections of ghosts.

Detach

Thank the stars for distances between
stars, for broad mountain meadows
that shrink your troubles to ants
carrying leaves five times their size.
The sun is 91 million miles away;
not too far, not too close. Be like that.
Perch in a look-out tower, overseer of campfires
and dangerous breezes. You'll spot the heat,
pick up the phone. Let others
put their faces in the fire.

Compost

"No woman should call another *fastidious*."
— James Thurber

She has in mind dahlias, a stretch
of dianthus, Jack-in-the-Pulpit or two.
For this, *rot*. In candid view!
Enough to make her retch—
the certainty of being touched, mussed,
dog-snouted till the prettiest sheen
turns brown, brown-black, black-green.
Once they called this mush *fastidious*.
Now it's the *woman's touch*, tight
as she flips a grub-infested
compost heap. Breath held, over-dressed
in fleece, gloves, clogs, apron, hat.
It's garden variety metamorphosis—
plain *disgust* to petal-perfect *daintiness*.

Bob White

Why the double bob, why the pause, as if pursing your tongue for the color. I have a friend who pauses like you, long enough to make the silence uncomfortable. I've learned to hold my tongue. I've seen you flying, ungraceful, like a hard boiled egg on a blue plate. The book says you like a fence rail, empty until you call. And then your bob, bobwhite, makes you appear closer than you really are. I would love to know: ratio of song volume to land claim. Why do you sing to this house? Perhaps you would like to live here. Land claim, a force mightier than sex— consider the number of men who died to save their wives. When you stop singing are you bored, angry, afraid, or . . . *thinking*? Bird brains are smaller than their eyes, though they store an extensive vocabulary. The grass switches and clicks with sparrows. They are multi-colored chips of steel, coarse ground pepper, staccato, pizzicato. They make me sneeze, which only intensifies their scolding. You are silent, Bob, assembling perhaps. "Perhaps" means I'm thinking. The fence is up for grabs.

A Ha Ha Fence

Sunken boundary to a garden, invisible until closely approached.

We dug a brick-lined trench
to ascertain, yet set our gardens free
from prim regularity. *Ha ha!* said one child
comprehending, mid-stride.
The other teetered, saved herself.

On Sundays, we leapt the ditch,
"All nature is a garden!" tasting the swell
and concave scoop. Our youngest
tossed a Frisbee, which we caught,
flipped back through the wood.

Praise be the landscape of subtle
intercession. We've avoided barbs,
mesh, hedges. Our outlook's truly fine,
a clear sweep to the horizon—
serene, maintenance-free.

Pond in Winter

A garden pond rimmed with stone
has frozen over, but under the ice
(like a soap-streaked shower curtain,
or distant light pollution),
a dozen goldfish churn the water
flourishing their Isadora fairy fins.
Above, a cat follows the orangey action,
pretend-yawns, skids, saunters
with sprawled claws. Winter insulates—
with just an inch of oxygen
the fish respire, feed, swim,
while our cat is a frenzy of gesture,
paws drumming: *You are going*
to die. If not now, in Spring, in Spring.

Three Sides to the Mountain That Are Really One

I.

In my dream I opened the mountain.
I don't mean sizzling gondola wires.
Or schuss marks like laugh lines
across Planplatte. I mean ran my nail
over the rock face and fell upon a rivet,
then a seam, then a curious counterfeit
moan. Under the neutral paint,
a hundred fighter planes.

2.

One night Frau Riemensberger
sliced up her husband with a paring knife
after she caught him peering
into the window of the girls' dorm.
She got off with a misdemeanor.
They always get off when the Föhn blows—
warm mountain wind, churning
ice into water, rock into soup,
reason into fog.

3.

I long for babies,
but never more than mountains.
My view of the Jungfrau: peaks like starched
petticoats I could bury my face in.
She is a cold confection, a meringue

I feel in my teeth. When I am
in the presence of mountains,
there will always be enough sex.
But never enough mountains.

Juncture

At the join
of sea to sky
a line of whitecaps
hovering

like a row of horseheads,
or ghost parapet
permeable

as in your dream
you glide
right up to the edge
the guardrail gives
undulates

you pass without harm
through a shark's teeth
and down
his smooth gullet

as of late when you lean
against your mother
and there's no

resistance—
she has stood firm
as long as she can

there at the horizon
where the clouds begin.

Lost

Woolen mittens
unfasten from a hand.
Loose and never photographed.
Dropped like peapods. Would you care
where a pod wound up, except to avoid
tossing it in your bed?

Try to remember! Ruthlessly clear
the gutter between your ears.
Move into a garden lean-to
and patch out the cirrus sky. (O lie
of infinite shelving. With all
we have to recall . . .)

The brain is a wicker basket,
confusion of peapods, photographs,
gloves lost, despite clips
and string threaded through sleeves.
Must have fallen out of the car.
Can't have gotten far.

Parting Prayer

Eternal God, charitable one
you have reluctantly included us
your back-up guest list
for the birthday of your Jesus Son
who will be two thousand ten
this December if the faithful
have it right. Over card table
and polka-dotted napkins,
over a feast of sourdough
and grape coolers in little plastic
shot glasses we beg you:
Is the tiremark over the puppy
(Route #1 out of Iowa City)
healed by now? Are feathers
on the woodpecker's head
grown back? She struck
our window *twice.* Any chance
our flesh persists in heaven?
If yes, send us out into the world
in peace, with party favors—
patience, thank yous,
gladness and singleness of heart,
at least until the far edge of your lawn,
miraculously pea-green in winter.
How do you do it—wave
friendly-host-like from the porch
trusting we'll cease
all ugly behavior, sweep
and disinfect under the bed,
love and serve you till the end,
to the glory of your Name. Amen.

Dusk

for Tom and Dodie

Consider dusk
draping the forest with a knit
shawl, that silences the free-for-all
and fashions for the aged
a sleeping place, yet knows to create
one last, delicious treat:
a red-eyed vireo, its song
swooping up like Mary Martin
to her lofty perch. Pleasure
like birdsong is sharper
when surrounded by lack.
We touch each other's faces in the dark
and the reason floats up slow—
why we married so long ago.

Floating City

In a field, festival pilots
nudge hot air balloons
upwards till the swells
rise like a dozen
multi-hued crocuses.

Blue, purple, Brut
and Cadillac-sponsored;
one whimsical masterpiece
shaped like a coconut
frosted cupcake. Seen from below

they are pre-teen
exclamation points.
The first riders were animal—
rooster, sheep, duck,
all pets. Wouldn't the sky

be just the place to live?
Floating city of primary
families, cousins in a chain
of smaller balloons
connected by ropes.

You'd have to work
to keep them close, Thanksgiving
a balancing act of buckets
pulleys and affectionate
hand signals. The air

full of seeds, tethers
forming a mist net
to catch stray geese. And rain
signals both drink
and frantic bailing.

No roads, train tracks,
runways, canals, bridges.
No place to be private,
unless desperate for love
you could slip inside

a cumulo-nimbus. That
would involve
great risk of course,
the dead merely synonym
for fallen.

This or That

This is the finger too stiff to bend, and the infant's clutching fist.

This the greasy bean before coffee.

This is the S curve, the tilt, and jump.

This is the light that will change, ungating cars like horses.

    (First signal, then turn.

    Remain in your seat. Caution: falling this, falling that.)

That man is not God, though he resembles a younger version.

This postcard comes from Jamaica.

That book, born on the Internet, takes place in Cambray.

    (Easier to imagine ghosts than real people in that dark.)

This chair we trust to comfort us, this spine we never consult.

    (Slippery when wet; not a leg to stand on.)

That Jiffy Lube, once a White Castle.

This valley view overspread with sadness, the tang of acetone.

This bundle, bending the twig.

That playground, till the bough broke.

This emergency your new life

depends on. This too shall pass.

On the Birth of a Daughter

You will be sleepless until you plant the Princess Tree.
Beloved for its architecture, large-hearted
foliage in whorls of lemon-green.

Rooted in peat, sand, or junk soil.
Two words for its adaptability:
Trash. Pioneer. Either way, it will survive a fire.

When your daughter matures, the tree must be sacrificed.
A phoenix will alight there
only when the queen steps down.

You must step down.

Acknowledgments

*American Poetry Review, Crazyhorse, Drunken Boat, Five Points,
Fourth Genre, Gettysburg Review, The Kenyon Review,
The Louisville Review, Open City, Poetry* ("Juncture"), *Pool,
Prairie Schooner, Southern Review, Virginia Quarterly Review,*
and *Wind.*

"Bust of a Young Girl in the Snow" appeared in
Best American Poetry 2006, edited by Billy Collins.

"Salon" was featured on *Poetry Daily.*

Special thanks to the Kentucky Arts Council,
the Kentucky Foundation for Women and, as ever, Jeffrey.

Sarah Gorham is the author of three previous collections of poetry: *The Cure* (2003), *The Tension Zone* (1996), and *Don't Go Back to Sleep* (1989). Individual poems have appeared in *Best American Poetry, American Poetry Review, Georgia Review, Kenyon Review, The Nation, Open City, Paris Review, Pool,* and elsewhere. She also writes essays, which have been published in *AGNI, Arts & Letters, Creative Nonfiction, Gulf Coast, Iowa Review,* and *Pleiades,* among other places. Gorham serves as editor-in-chief of Sarabande Books, which she co-founded in 1994. She lives in Prospect, Kentucky, with her husband, the poet Jeffrey Skinner.